MYSTERIES OF SCIENCE

ALIEN ABDUCTIONS
THE UNSOLVED MYSTERY

BY LISA WADE McCORMICK

Reading Consultant:
Barbara J. Fox
Reading Specialist
North Carolina State University

Content Consultant:
Andrew Nichols, PhD
Executive Director
American Institute of Parapsychology
Gainesville, Florida

Capstone
press

Mankato, Minnesota

Blazers is published by Capstone Press,
151 Good Counsel Drive, P.O. Box 669, Mankato, Minnesota 56002.
www.capstonepress.com

Books published by Capstone Press are manufactured with paper
containing at least 10 percent post-consumer waste.

Library of Congress Cataloging-in-Publication Data
McCormick, Lisa Wade, 1961–
    Alien abductions : the unsolved mystery/ by Lisa Wade McCormick.
    p. cm. — (Blazers. Mysteries of science)
    Includes bibliographical references and index.
    Summary: "Presents the mystery of alien abductions, including current theories and famous
abduction stories" — Provided by publisher.
    ISBN: 978-1-4296-3393-2 (library binding)
    1. Alien abduction — Juvenile literature. 2. Human-alien encounters — Juvenile literature.
I. Title. II. Series.
BF2050.M38 2010
001.942 — dc22   2009005055

Editorial Credits
Katy Kudela, editor; Alison Thiele, set designer; Heidi Thompson, book designer;
    Svetlana Zhurkin, media researcher

Photo Credits
Alamy/Carol and Mike Werner, 26
Capstone Press/Karon Dubke, 20–21
Corbis/Bettmann, 8–9
Fortean Picture Library, 4–5, 12–13, 28–29
Getty Images/Hulton Archive, 18–19
iStockphoto/Lee Pettet, 23
Mary Evans Picture Library, cover, 6–7, 10–11, 14–15, 24–25
Shutterstock/Drobova, (image bullets) 16–17; Marilyn Volan, grunge background (throughout);
    Maugli, 16–17 (background); rgbspace, (paper art element) 3, 17; Shmeliova Natalia, 16
    (paper art element)

TABLE OF CONTENTS

ALIEN ENCOUNTER?

A husband and wife see a flying spaceship. They hear strange beeping sounds. Two hours suddenly pass. They do not remember what happened.

ALIEN FACT

In 2000, a study showed that 33 percent of Americans believe strange beings are visiting Earth.

6

Soon after that strange night, the wife has **nightmares**. The wife dreams that **aliens** take her and her husband to a spaceship. She begins to think her dreams are actually memories of the strange night.

nightmare — a bad dream
alien — a creature from another planet

What happened to Betty and
Barney Hill on September 19, 1961?
Did Betty just have bad dreams?
Or did aliens **abduct** them?

abduct — to take someone away by force

ALIEN FACT

Pease Air Force Base in New Hampshire spotted a flying object. The object appeared the night the Hills say they saw a spacecraft.

ALIEN ABDUCTIONS

Thousands of people believe they have met aliens. Some say aliens took them to their spaceships.

ALIEN FACT

Australian Kelly Cahill said aliens took her in August 1993. A family said they saw Cahill being taken.

Some people have reported that aliens took them from their homes or cars. They claim aliens came through walls and windows. Others say that aliens appeared in a beam of light.

ALIEN FACT

People who claim they have met aliens also say they lost time. They can't remember parts of their day.

13

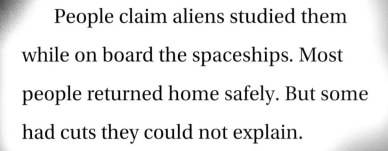

People claim aliens studied them while on board the spaceships. Most people returned home safely. But some had cuts they could not explain.

ALIEN FACT

Some people think aliens put objects in human bodies to track them.

FAMOUS ALIEN ENCOUNTERS

- Antonio Villas Boas of Brazil claimed four aliens took him in 1957. He said they took blood from his chin. Before leaving the spaceship, Boas tried to take an object. The aliens would not let him leave with proof.

- Travis Walton of Arizona said aliens took him on November 5, 1975. He said a beam of light lifted him into a spaceship. Some co-workers claim they saw the strange event. Walton was missing for five days.

Linda Napolitano of New York said aliens took her to their spaceship in 1989. Several people said they saw Napolitano float into a flying ship. None of these people knew her.

In September 1994, children in Zimbabwe, Africa, said they saw aliens in their school yard. All 62 children drew pictures of aliens with large heads. Before this event, these children had never seen pictures of aliens.

STUDYING ABDUCTIONS

People want to find out if alien abductions are real. Scientists and other people study **UFO** sightings and alien abductions.

UFO — an object in the sky thought to be a spaceship from another planet

EXCHANGE BUILDINGS

In 1953, a UFO was spotted in the sky in Zimbabwe.

Researchers talk to people who believe they have met aliens. Researchers use **hypnosis** to help people remember what happened.

researcher — someone who studies a subject to discover new information

hypnosis — a method used to put people in a sleeplike state

People who say they have been taken tell the same kind of story. They say strange beings took them to a spaceship. Some claim these aliens had big heads and huge black eyes.

ALIEN FACT

Many people claim to have met aliens called Greys. They say these short aliens have big heads and tiny mouths.

23

ABDUCTIONS OR DREAMS?

Most scientists do not believe in alien abductions. They say there is no proof. There are no photos of aliens. No one has brought back an object from a spaceship.

Scientists say people who have waking dreams may think aliens have taken them. These dreams happen when people start to wake up. They may imagine flashing lights or scary beings.

ALIEN FACT

Most people say they were fully awake when they were taken by aliens.

27

What do you think? Have aliens taken people? No one knows for sure. Scientists and researchers will continue to search for the answer.

GLOSSARY

abduct (ab-DUKT) — to take someone away by force

alien (AY-lee-uhn) — a creature from another planet

hypnosis (hip-NOH-sis) — a method used to put people in a sleeplike state in which they answer questions and easily respond to different suggestions

nightmare (NITE-mair) — a frightening or unpleasant dream or experience

proof (PROOF) — facts or evidence that something is true

researcher (REE-surch-ur) — someone who studies a subject to discover new information

UFO (YOO EF OH) — an object in the sky thought to be a spaceship from another planet; UFO is short for Unidentified Flying Object.

READ MORE

Miller, Connie Colwell. *UFOs: The Unsolved Mystery.*
Mysteries of Science. Mankato, Minn.: Capstone Press, 2009.

Rooney, Anne. *Alien Abduction.* Crabtree Contact.
New York: Crabtree, 2008.

Walker, Kathryn. *Mysteries of Alien Visitors and Abductions.*
Unsolved! New York: Crabtree, 2009.

INTERNET SITES

FactHound offers a safe, fun way to find Internet sites
related to this book. All of the sites on FactHound
have been researched by our staff.

Here's all you do:

Visit *www.facthound.com*

FactHound will fetch the best sites for you!

INDEX